Eric

Francine

Gary

a b c d e f g h i j k l m n o p q r s t u v w x y z a b c d e f g h i

my first

Debbie MacKinnon

photographs by Anthea Sieveking

BARRON'S

Xanthe

Yolanda

Zachary

Alison's apple

Brian's book

Cathy's car

David's doll

Eric's elephant

Francine's
frog

Gary's guitar

Henry's house

Isabel's
ice cream

Jennifer's jack-in-the-box

Kevin's **k**angaroo

Lee's ladybug

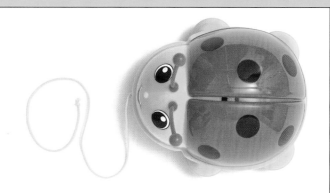

Max's mobile

Nick's
numbers

Oliver's
oranges

Polly's pool

Quentin's quilt

Rachel's rabbit

Sophie's sandbox

Tom's
teddy

Ursula's umbrella

Victor's vacuum cleaner

Wendy's wheelbarrow

Xanthe's
xylophone

Yolanda's yacht

Zachary's zebra

For my parents – D. M.
For Margaret – A. S.

First edition for the United States and Canada
published 1992 by Barron's Educational Series, Inc.
Text copyright © Debbie MacKinnon 1992
Illustrations copyright © Anthea Sieveking 1992

First published in Great Britain in 1992 by
Frances Lincoln Limited, Apollo Works
5 Charlton Kings Road, London NW5 2SB

All inquiries should be addressed to:
Barron's Educational Series, Inc.
250 Wireless Boulevard
Hauppauge, NY 11788

Library of Congress Catalog Card No. 92 – 11500

International Standard Book No. 0-8120-6331-7

Library of Congress Cataloging-in-Publication Data
MacKinnon, Debbie.
    My first ABC / Debbie MacKinnon : photographs by Anthea Sieveking.
  —1st ed.
        p.   cm.
    Summary: Photographs represent the alphabet from A to Z.
    ISBN 0-8120-6331-7
    1. English language—Alphabet—Juvenile literature.
[1. Alphabet.] I. Sieveking, Anthea, ill.   II. Title.
PE1155.M345   1992
[E]—dc20   92-11500
                                                                                    CIP
                                                                                    AC

Design and art direction by Debbie MacKinnon

Printed and bound in Hong Kong

2 3 4 5   9 8 7 6 5 4 3 2 1